Sophie Ryan

energy balls

30 Simple And Delicious Superfood Energy Balls And Bites Recipes For Great Health and Wellbeing

Text and illustration copyright © 2016 Erin Rose Publishing

Design: Julie Anson

ISBN:978-0-9933204-7-7

A CIP record for this book is available from the British Library.

All Rights Reserved. No part of this publication may be reproduced, stored in a retrieval system or transmitted by any form or by any means, electronic, recording or otherwise without the prior permission in writing from the publishers. Unauthorised reproduction of any part of this publication by any means including photocopying is an infringement of copyright.

DISCLAIMER: This book is for informational purposes only and not intended as a substitute for the medical advice, diagnosis or treatment of a physician or qualified healthcare provider. The reader should consult a physician before undertaking a new health care regime and in all matters relating to his/her health, and particularly with respect to any symptoms that may require diagnosis or medical attention.

While every care has been taken in compiling the recipes for this book we cannot accept responsibility for any problems which arise as a result of preparing one of the recipes. The author and publisher disclaim responsibility for any adverse effects that may arise from the use or application of the recipes in this book. Some of the recipes in this book include nuts. If you have a nut allergy it is important to avoid these.

contents

Power Balls That Pack A Punch!

If you are looking for healthy and delicious snacks that are full of goodness, look no further! Energy Balls are packed with nature's 'super foods' and are just the snack to give you a powerful nutritious boost at any time of the day! These wonder foods provide you with the benefits of wholesome nutritious super foods packed into one tasty delicious ball, ideal for on-the-go snacks, a quick energy boost before the gym or a lunch box treat for the kids.

In this book, there are 30 recipes for naturally healthy energy balls which are high in protein, dairy-free, vegetarian and contain no added sugar so you can be sure you get a boost of vitamins and minerals without unnecessary additives, so you and your family can enjoy these delicious super food balls of guilt-free pleasure!

Each of these sweet and savoury recipes contain ingredients which are great for your health. We know that some lesser-known, nutrient-rich foods can be expensive, which is why we've included recipes which are made with common store-cupboard ingredients, so there really is something for everyone! There is no need to be put off by ingredients you've never heard off – you can make energy balls with a few core basics. Once you know how to make energy balls, you can have fun experimenting with your own favourite ingredients!

Superstar Superfoods

We've selected ingredients from top 'superfoods' combining common healthy, store cupboard ingredients with less well-known super nutrient foods which make healthy eating accessible. Below are the top foods we've included in our energy balls recipes, so you can top up your diet with additional nutrients. Once you've had a look at the recipes you can stock up your cupboards with some of these essentials. While there are numerous organic plant powders and protein powder supplements on the market which boost your nutrient intake, they obviously aren't a substitute for a healthy diet. However, they do make a great addition to energy balls and adding them to recipes is a great way of incorporating them into your diet.

Almonds

Avocado

Beetroot

Brazil Nuts

Broccoli

Cannellini Beans

Cashew nuts

Chia Seeds

Cocoa/Dark Chocolate

Coconut & Coconut oil

Dates

Dried Apricots

Goji Berries

Hemp Seeds

Kale

Lentils

Linseeds (Flaxseeds)

Macadamia nuts

Oats

Peanuts

Pistachios

Plant powders: matcha, maca, baobab, spirulina etc

Pumpkin Seeds

Quinoa

Sesame Seeds

Sweet Potato

Turmeric

Walnuts

What Superfoods Can Do For You

There's no doubt that adding natural super foods can revitalise your energy, helping you achieve greater well-being and vitality. In this section we look at a few of the ingredients we've used, to show you why adding these delicious ingredients can really kick-start your healthy regime and provide nutritional support to your everyday diet.

Avocados

An avocado's creamy flesh is literally packed with health promoting nutrients. Until recently, dieters have avoided avocados due to concern about their high monounsaturated fat content. However the steady energy release and the feeling of satiety and fullness that comes from eating healthy fats like an avocado actually helps by reducing your appetite and avoiding hunger pangs. Research has shown that avocado's monounsaturated fatty acids are much more likely to be used as slow burning energy than stored as body fat.

Avocados also provide many vitamins and minerals, including vitamin B, vitamin K, iron, folate, potassium, beta-carotene and lutein. Avocados contain high levels of monounsaturated fats, phytosterols and antioxidants like vitamin E, and vitamin C and can help reduce the inflammation that leads to chronic illnesses like arthritis.

Beetroot

Research has shown that eating beetroot can boost the levels of antioxidants in the body and it's traditionally been used to assist diseases of the liver and help with the body's detoxification ability. Beetroot has also been hailed as an excellent blood tonic, improving the immune system's ability to deal with abnormal cells. It is also a rich source of fibre, which is essential for healthy cholesterol, maintaining a healthy digestive tract and promoting all round good health.

Chia Seeds

These can be found in the whole foods section of most supermarkets. These tiny little seeds are low in carbohydrates and expand with moisture to become a gel-like texture. This leads to a need for fewer calories, by creating a feeling of fullness by the fibre in the seeds. The fibre also helps maintain a healthy gut flora, so they are worth including in your diet.

Cocoa

Chocolate is good for you! Great news for chocolate lovers, but don't reach for a chocolate bar just yet! Raw cacao is far superior with the benefits it offers because of its high nutrient content. The important thing to remember when selecting chocolate is to make sure it has a high cocoa content and to avoid sugary chocolate bars, which offer no nutritional benefit. The cocoa bean was used by the Mayans for its psychological, health and well-being effects and modern science now acknowledges that high quality chocolate is beneficial as the flavonoids in cacao increase the blood flow and oxygen to the brain. Cocoa is bursting with a supply of antioxidants which help ward off chronic illnesses. Cocoa also contains potassium, phosphorus, copper, zinc, iron and magnesium which contribute to cardiovascular health. Chocolate triggers the release of the endorphin dopamine which lifts the mood and relieves stress.

Another benefit of chocolate is that it's a 'sirt food' which activates your SIRT1 gene, also known as your 'skinny gene' which benefits cell renewal while boosting your metabolism.

Coconut & Coconut Oil

Coconut is high in dietary fibre and has a low glycemic index (GI) so it has little effect on the body's blood sugar as it slowly releases energy. It also requires less insulin for the cells to use the glucose, therefore relieving stress on the body. This means that it's a great weight loss food which staves off sugar cravings. It's helpful for the digestive tract as it provides amino acids, vitamins and minerals which are easily absorbed, whilst providing a super boost of energy.

Coconut oil is now commonly used for cosmetic purposes to improve the appearance of hair and skin, but the benefits of coconut oil are more far reaching. When coconut oil is digested, it not only provides a welcome source of energy for the body but it forms monolaurin which combats viruses, bacteria and fungi, so it's particularly useful in the treatment of infections in the body.

Dates

Dates can have a laxative effect, therefore they can relieve constipation and intestinal disorders due to their high fibre content. They are a delicious and naturally sweet way of adding calcium, potassium, phosphorous, manganese, copper and magnesium to your diet. They're also high in iron so very useful if you are anaemic. Like chocolate, they are also a 'sirt food', which triggers metabolic and cell function benefits.

Goji Berries

The goji berry is a dried, bright red-orange berry originating from China and they've long been used in traditional Chinese medicine to help manage high blood pressure, diabetes and fever. Goji berries contain vitamin C, vitamin B2, vitamin A, iron, selenium and other antioxidants. Antioxidants combat destructive free radicals which cause cell destruction and accelerated ageing, so these berries are a wonderful addition to your diet. Similar to other berries, goji berries are also high in beta-carotene which promotes healthy skin. A little word of caution though; check with your GP or pharmacist if you are on medication for diabetes or blood thinning medication, before adding goji berries to your diet.

Hemp

Hemp seeds are a fabulous addition to your diet and are a valuable protein food source, containing essential amino acids which provide numerous health benefits as they aid good digestion, help build muscle mass, treat insomnia, anaemia and build healthy bones, skin and hair. This means that it contains all 8 essential amino acids that the body cannot produce naturally, but requires for a vast number of internal processes.

Honey

Raw honey, which hasn't been heated beyond 40c, has medicinal benefits for the digestion and wound healing. Manuka honey contains antibacterial and antifungal properties which promote healing and assists the immune system.

Oats

Oats contain beta-glucans, a type of soluble fibre that slows down digestion and prevents dramatic spikes in blood sugar. Oats are rich in magnesium which is essential for energy production, maintaining healthy blood pressure and preventing heart attacks and strokes. It's believed there is also a link between low magnesium levels and depression.

Nuts & Seeds

Nuts and seeds are power houses of nutrition, providing protein, essential fatty acids and antioxidants such as resveratrol, carotenes and lutein which can help protect against chronic illnesses. They not only contain a protein rich calorie boost but they contain B vitamins which are important for the nervous system, metabolism and converting food to energy. They are a rich source of minerals like iron, manganese, potassium, calcium, magnesium, zinc and selenium. Potassium regulates fluids that help control heart rate and blood pressure. Nuts are also a wonderful source of vitamin E which is required to maintain healthy skin, protecting the body from harmful free radicals.

Nuts are a rich source of omega-3 essential fatty acids and provide anti-inflammatory benefits, helping lower the risk of heart disease, strokes and rheumatoid arthritis. Almonds are rich in calcium, which is great news for anyone avoiding dairy produce, plus their vitamin E content is great for your skin. Brazil nuts are rich in selenium which helps the immune system and the thyroid gland.

For anyone concerned about the fat content of nuts, remember that they contain healthy fats which your body thrives on.

Always try and buy your nuts as fresh as you can, or store them in an airtight container for a short time only, as they can turn rancid.

Super-Nutrient Plant Powders

There are a wide variety of plant-based nutrient powders to choose from and the price can sometimes be the only drawback. In this book we've included the use of powders such as matcha, acai, baobab, maca and spirulina to really pack in the vitamins, fibre and nutrients. However, you can still make wonderfully healthy and delicious energy balls without them. The variety available also includes; moringa, super greens, chlorella, lucuma, pea protein, wheatgrass and camu powder. If you are using chlorella powder, it's advisable to use the cracked-cell variety as you can experience digestive upsets otherwise. The benefits of plant protein and plant nutrient powders are many and varied and will add extra nutrition to your energy balls.

Sweet Potatoes

Their natural sweetness makes them a versatile ingredient, not only as a replacement for the humble potato but they can be used in dessert recipes to add natural sweetness and flavour. Sweet potatoes are a rich source of antioxidants and they help to regulate blood sugar.

recipes

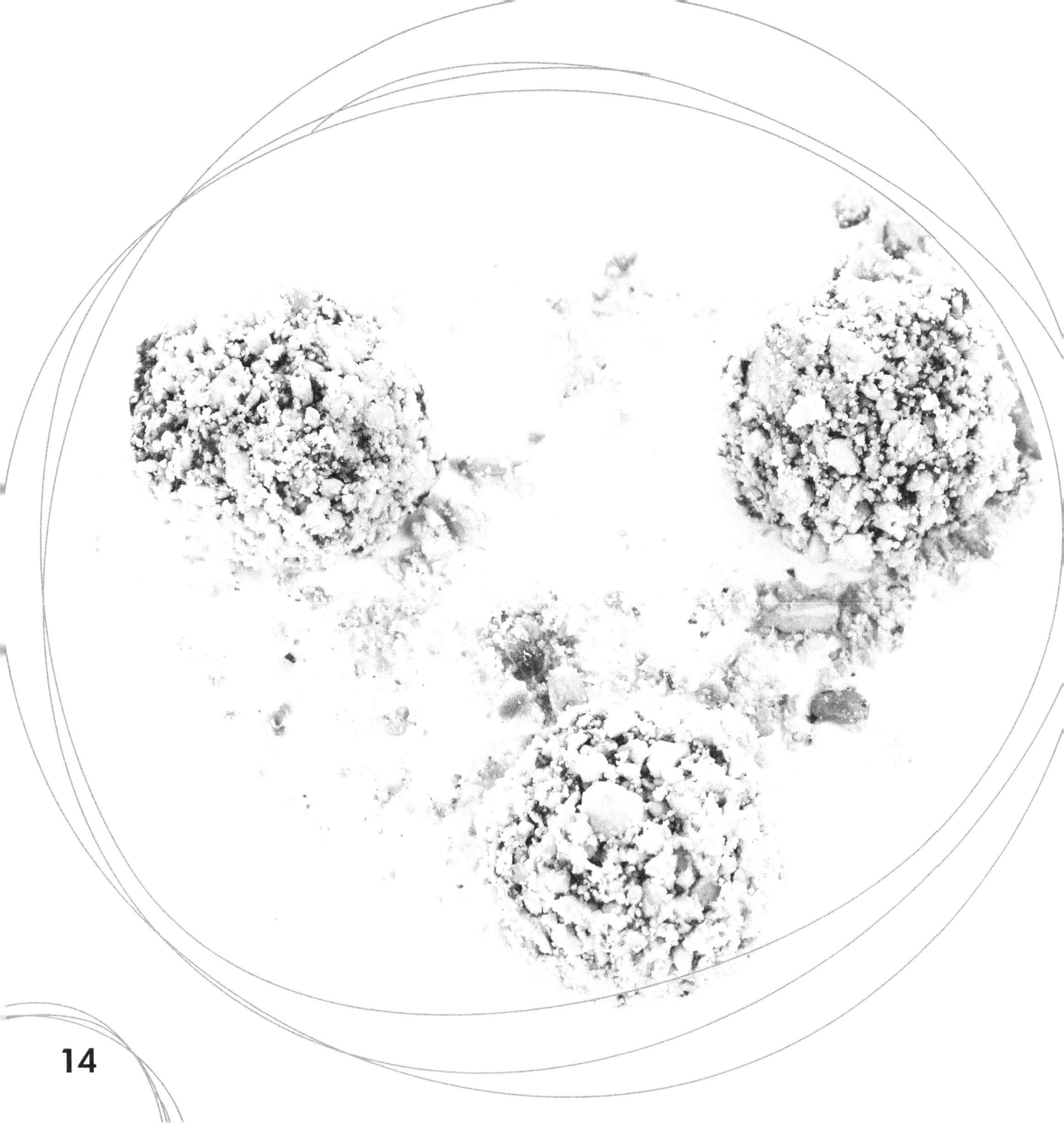

Chocolate Chip & Peanut Vitality Boosts

Ingredients

150g (5oz) pitted dates, chopped
150g (5oz) pumpkin seeds (or sunflower seeds)
50g (2oz) cacao nibs
25g (1oz) 100% cocoa powder
25g (1oz) unsalted peanuts, finely chopped
2 tablespoons water (optional)
1 teaspoon vanilla extract
Pinch of sea salt

Method

Place the pumpkin seeds, cocoa powder, vanilla extract and salt in a food processor and process until fine. Add in the dates and blend to a sticky consistency. Transfer the mixture to a bowl and add in some water if you need to make the dough softer. Stir in the cacao nibs then roll the mixture into individual bite-size balls. Place the chopped peanuts on a plate and roll the balls in them to completely cover them. Store in an airtight container if you manage not to eat them all straight away! Enjoy.

Cherry & Coconut Bites

Ingredients

100g ($3\frac{1}{2}$ oz) oats
50g (2oz) desiccated (shredded) coconut
50g (2oz) peanut butter
50g (2oz) dried cherries
50g (2oz) sunflower seeds
2 tablespoons raw honey
3 tablespoons ground linseeds (flaxseeds)

Method

Place all of the ingredients in a bowl and mix the ingredients together really well. Cover it and allow it to sit for 30 minutes, ready to be rolled into bite-size balls. If the mixture seems too dry to stick together, add a tablespoon or two of water to help it bind together. Shape the mixture into individual balls. Store them in an airtight container until you are ready to eat them.

Brazil & Chocolate Goji Vitality Bursts

Ingredients

150g (5oz) pitted dates
100g (3½ oz) brazil nuts
75g (3oz) cacao nibs or 100% cocoa powder
50g (2oz) linseeds (flaxseeds)
50g (2oz) sesame seeds
50g (2oz) goji berries
50g (2oz) desiccated (shredded) coconut
1½ teaspoons ground cinnamon
1 tablespoon maca powder
2 tablespoons raw honey

MAKES approx. 24

Method

Place the linseeds (flaxseeds), sesame seeds, brazil nuts, and cacao nibs/cocoa powder into a food processor and blend until it is fine. Add in the goji berries, dates, maca powder, cinnamon, coconut and honey and blitz until you have a sticky paste. Scoop out the mixture and roll into bite-size balls. Store them in an airtight container in the fridge until ready to use – if you can wait!

Cranberry & Raisin Power Balls

Ingredients

100g (3½ oz) oats
50g (2oz) almond butter
25g (1oz) ground linseeds (flaxseeds)
1 tablespoon dried cranberries
1 tablespoon raisins
1 tablespoon maca powder
3 pitted dates
½ teaspoon ground cinnamon

Method

Place the oats, linseeds (flaxseeds), cranberries, maca powder and cinnamon in a bowl. Place the almond butter, raisins and dates into a food processor and blitz until they are combined. Add the date mixture to the dry ingredients and mix well. Shape the mixture into individual balls of around 2.5cm (1 inch) in size. Store them in an airtight container or freeze them until you need them.

Almond & Spirulina Treats

Ingredients

150g (5oz) almonds
100g (3½oz) dates, soaked in water for 30 minutes then drained
25g (1oz) dried apricots, finely chopped
25g (1oz) pistachio nuts
25g (1oz) almond butter
2 tablespoons 100% cocoa powder
2 tablespoons linseeds (flaxseeds)
2 tablespoons desiccated (shredded) coconut
1 tablespoon spirulina powder
Extra coconut for rolling

MAKES approx. 24

Method

Place all of the pistachio nuts, almonds and flaxseeds into a food processor and process until fine. Place the apricots and dates in a bowl and add in the ground nuts from the food processor. Mix them well. Add in the almond butter, cocoa powder, coconut and spirulina and stir to combine until everything is mixed thoroughly. Shape the mixture into balls. Scatter some desiccated (shredded) coconut on a large plate and roll the balls in it, coating them thoroughly. Store in an airtight container or freeze them for a handy on-the-go snack if you manage not to eat them all straight away! Enjoy.

Fruit & Nut Breakfast Balls

MAKES approx. 24

Ingredients

100g (3½ oz) rolled oats
100g (3½ oz) dried apricots
100g (3½ oz) dried fig
100g (3½ oz) dried apple rings, chopped
50g (2oz) cashew nuts, chopped
50g (2oz) sunflower seeds, chopped
2 tablespoons tahini (sesame seed paste)
60mls (2fl oz) fresh apple juice (not concentrated)

Method

Place the dried fruit into a blender and process until roughly chopped. Add in the oats, seeds and nuts and process until chunky but mixed well. Add in the tahini and apple juice and combine. Shape the mixture into balls and lay them on a baking sheet. (Alternatively you can press the mixture into a shallow rectangular dish to make breakfast bars). Transfer the balls to the oven and bake at 190C/375F for 20-25 minutes. These not only make a great on-the-go breakfast but are a delicious snack too.

Chocolate Cashew Bites

Ingredients

125g (4oz) unsalted cashew nuts
50g (2oz) almonds
14 pitted dates, finely chopped
2 tablespoons 100% cocoa powder
1 tablespoon baobab powder (optional)
1 tablespoon coconut oil

Method

Place all of the ingredients into a food processor and mix until they are thoroughly combined. Shape the mixture into balls and store them in an airtight container in the fridge until you're ready to serve.

Apricot & Almond Truffles

Ingredients

150g (5oz) almonds
150g (5oz) dried apricots
75g (3oz) raisins
2 tablespoons pumpkin seeds
1 tablespoon baobab powder
1 tablespoon coconut oil
1 tablespoon desiccated (shredded) coconut
1 tablespoon water (optional)
Extra coconut for rolling

Method

Place all the ingredients into a food processor and mix until chunky and sticky. Scoop out a spoonful of mixture and roll it into a ball. Repeat for the remaining mixture. You can add a tablespoon of water if the mixture needs extra moisture. Scatter some coconut on a plate and roll the balls in it. Store them in an airtight container.

Creamy Avocado Chocolate Bites

MAKES approx. 14

Ingredients

75g (3oz) dark chocolate, minimum 80% cocoa or cacao nibs
3 avocados, flesh removed
1 teaspoon vanilla extract
1 tablespoon honey (or ½ -1 teaspoon stevia powder) (optional)
Pinch of salt
100% cocoa powder for rolling

Method

Place the chocolate and honey/stevia in a large bowl and place it over a saucepan of gently simmering water until the chocolate has melted. Add in the vanilla and salt and stir. Mash the avocado until it is smooth and creamy. Pour the melted chocolate into the mashed avocado and mix it thoroughly. Chill in the fridge for 30 minutes until it becomes thicker. Using a teaspoon, scoop out the mixture and roll it into balls. Place the cocoa powder for rolling on a plate and completely coat the chocolate balls in the mixture. Serve and enjoy.

Cinnamon & Fig Power Bites

Ingredients

150g (5oz) dried figs
100g (3½oz) shelled hemp seeds
3 tablespoons maca powder
½ teaspoon cinnamon
Pinch of salt
Hemp seeds for garnish

Method

Place all of the ingredients into a blender and process until the mixture becomes a soft dough. You can add a tablespoon or two or water if the mixture seems too thick. Using your hands, roll the mixture into balls. Sprinkle some hemp seeds on a plate and roll the balls in it. Serve and enjoy.

Zesty Lime & Coconut Energy Balls

Ingredients

200g (7oz) pitted dates
100g (3½ oz) almonds
25g (1oz) cashew nuts
Zest and juice of 3 limes
Desiccated (shredded) coconut for rolling

Method

Place the cashew nuts and almonds into a food processor and blend to a fine powder. Add in the dates, lime juice and zest and process until the mixture is sticky. Roll the mixture into balls. Scatter the desiccated (shredded) coconut on a plate and roll the balls in it until they are well coated. These are refreshing and delicious!

Carrot Cake Balls

Ingredients

125g (4oz) oats
25g (1oz) coconut flour
4 pitted dates
3 dried apricots
1 medium carrot, peeled and finely grated (finely shredded)
1 teaspoon maca powder
1 teaspoon vanilla extract
½ teaspoon cinnamon
¼ teaspoon ground ginger
¼ teaspoon ground nutmeg
Desiccated (shredded) coconut for rolling

Method

Place all of the ingredients into a food processor and mix until thoroughly combined. Roll the mixture into individual balls. If the mixture seems too dry you can try adding a tablespoon or two or water to help it stick together. Scatter the extra coconut on a large plate and coat the carrot cake balls in it. Store in an airtight container.

Pistachio & Matcha Balls

Ingredients

200g (7oz) pistachio nuts
100g (3½ oz) pitted dates
100g (3½ oz) dried apricots, chopped
100g (3½ oz) pumpkin seeds
50g (2oz) desiccated coconut
1 teaspoon matcha powder
1 teaspoon acai powder
2 tablespoons tahini paste (sesame seed paste)
½ teaspoon vanilla essence
1-2 tablespoons water (optional)
Extra coconut for rolling

Method

Place the pistachio nuts, acai, matcha, pumpkin seeds and coconut into a food processor and mix until combined. Add in the dates and apricots and process until slightly chunky. Add in the vanilla essence and tahini paste and stir. The mixture should be fairly sticky but add a tablespoon or two or water if it seems too dry. Roll the mixture into bite-size balls. Scatter the coconut onto a large plate and roll the balls in it. Enjoy.

Ginger & Coconut Energy Balls

Ingredients

125g (4oz) pitted dates, chopped
100g (3½ oz) desiccated (shredded) coconut
75g (3oz) brazil nuts, chopped
2.5cm (1inch) chunk fresh ginger root, peeled and chopped
Finely chopped brazil nuts for rolling

Method

Place all of the ingredients into a blender and process until well combined and sticky. Shape the mixture into balls and add a little water to make it easier if necessary. Scatter the brazil nuts onto a plate and roll the balls in it. Store them in an airtight container or devour them straight away!

Coffee Fitness Bursts

Ingredients

275g (10oz) pitted dates
4 tablespoons 100% cocoa powder
2 tablespoons ground almonds
2 teaspoons cinnamon
2 tablespoons almond butter
3 tablespoons black brewed coffee

Method

Place all of the ingredients into a blender and process until the mixture becomes thick and chunky. Shape the mixture into ball shapes and store them in an airtight container. These are a great snack before a workout to give you a boost. They can even be frozen, ready to be used as a time-saving snack.

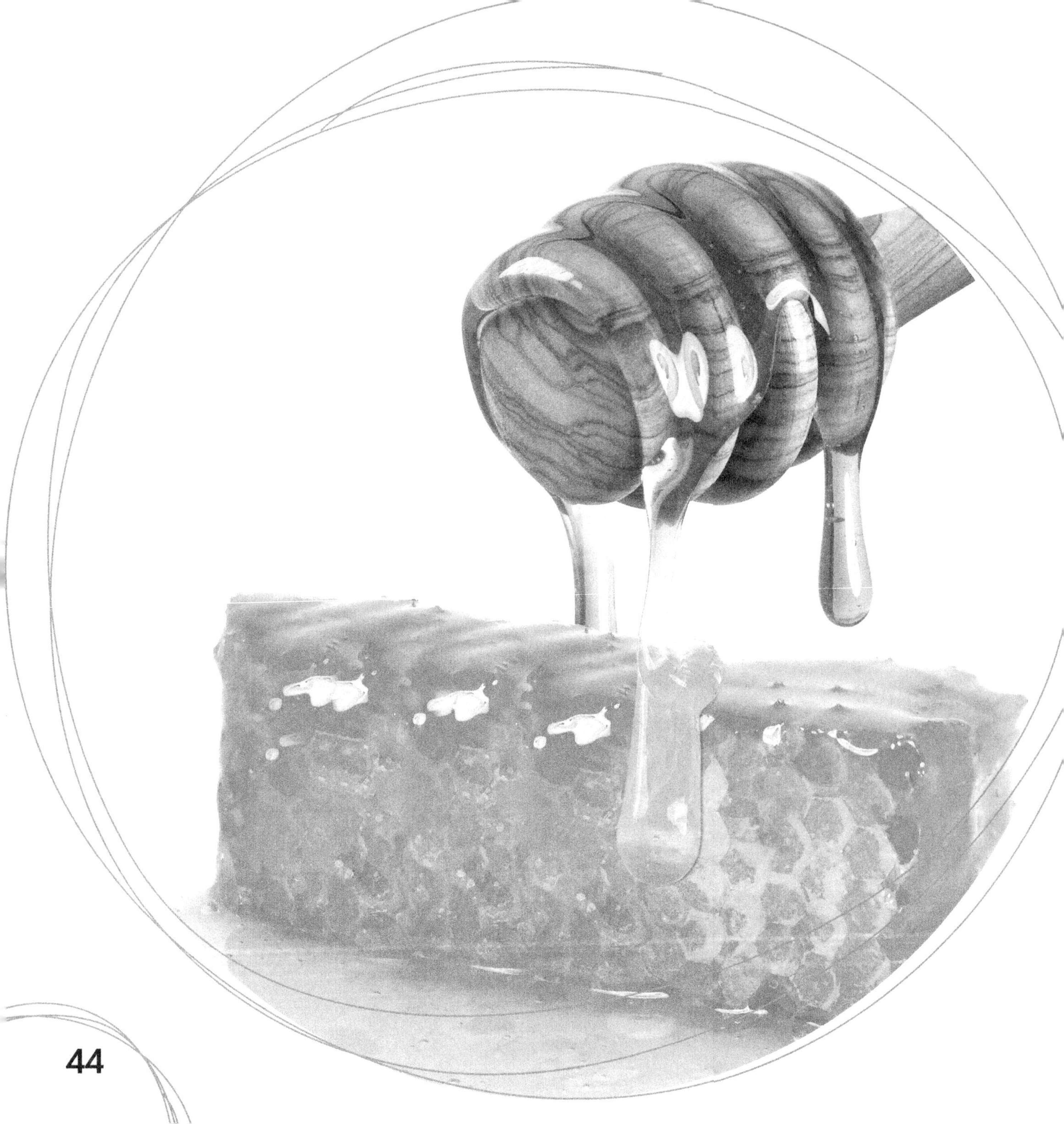

Supreme Superfood Balls

Ingredients

100g (3½ oz) almond butter
100g (3½ oz) brown rice puffs
100g (3½ oz) desiccated (shredded) coconut
75g (3oz) oats
50g (2oz) shelled hemp seeds
1 teaspoon maca powder
1 teaspoon spirulina powder
4 tablespoons raw honey (or brown rice syrup)
Pinch of sea salt
Shelled hemp seeds for rolling

Method

Place the almond butter, honey (or brown rice syrup) maca powder, spirulina and salt in a bowl and mix it thoroughly. Add in the coconut, oats, hemp seeds and rice puffs and combine all the ingredients. Shape the mixture into balls. Scatter some hulled hemp seeds on a plate and coat the balls in them. Store in a refrigerator until ready to use.

Lemon & Blueberry Energy Bites

Ingredients

225g (8oz) cashew nuts
100g (3½ oz) pitted dates
75g (3oz) dried blueberries
50g (2oz) desiccated (shredded) coconut
2 tablespoons lemon juice
1 teaspoon matcha powder
1 teaspoon lemon zest
Extra coconut and a little chopped lemon zest for rolling

Method

Place the coconut and cashew nuts into a food processor and blitz until fine. Add in the matcha powder, dates, dried blueberries, lemon juice, and zest and process to a doughy consistency. Roll the mixture into balls. Scatter the coconut and lemon zest onto a plate and roll the balls in it. Enjoy straight away or store in the fridge.

Almond Chocolate Truffles

Ingredients

100g (3½ oz) pitted dates
75g (3oz) almonds
75g (30z) walnuts
25g (1oz) desiccated (shredded) coconut
3 tablespoons maca powder
3 tablespoons 100% cacao powder
1 teaspoon ground cinnamon
1 tablespoon coconut oil
1-2 tablespoons water (optional)
Desiccated (shredded) coconut for rolling

Method

Place the almonds and walnuts in a food processor and blend until they become fine. Add in the remaining ingredients and process until the mixture becomes doughy. You can add a little water if the mixture is too dry to stick. Roll the mixture into bite-size balls. Scatter the desiccated (shredded) coconut on a plate and roll the energy balls in it, coating them completely. As an alternative you could even press a whole almond onto the top of each ball.

Goji & Cashew Power Balls

Ingredients

100g (3½ oz) desiccated coconut flakes
125g (4oz) unsalted cashew nuts
125g (4oz) goji berries
125mls (4fl oz) melted coconut oil
2 tablespoons raw honey
1 tablespoon baobab powder
Pinch of sea salt
Extra coconut and a little baobab powder for dusting (optional)

Method

Place all of the ingredients into a food processor and process until it becomes a soft consistency. Roll the mixture into balls. Sprinkle some coconut and baobab powder, if you are using, onto a plate and coat the balls in it. Store in an airtight container in the fridge until ready to eat. As they contain coconut oil, they can melt at room temperature.

Cinnamon & Chia Bites

MAKES approx. 24

Ingredients

225g (8oz) pitted dates
125g (4oz) almonds
2 tablespoons almond butter
2 tablespoons coconut oil
2 tablespoons maca powder
2 tablespoons chia seeds
1 tablespoon raw honey
1 teaspoon ground cinnamon

Method

Place the almonds in a food processor and blitz until fine. Add in the maca powder, dates, chia seeds and cinnamon and blend until the mixture becomes sticky. Add in the almond butter, coconut oil, honey. Using clean hands, roll the mixture into bite size balls. Keep them refrigerated before serving.

Cashew, Raisin & Baobab Truffles

Ingredients

150g (5oz) raisins
125g (4oz) cashew nuts
2 tablespoons chia seeds
1 tablespoon coconut oil
1 tablespoon peanut butter (or other nut butter)
1 tablespoon baobab powder
1 tablespoon cocoa powder
Extra cocoa powder for rolling

Method

Place the cashew nuts into a blender and process until they are a fine powder. Add the remaining ingredients and process until the mixture is soft and sticky. Shape the mixture into small ball shapes. Scatter some cocoa powder onto a plate and roll the truffles in it. Store them in a container and keep them in the fridge, ready to use. If you wish you can roll them in a little baobab powder instead of cocoa powder.

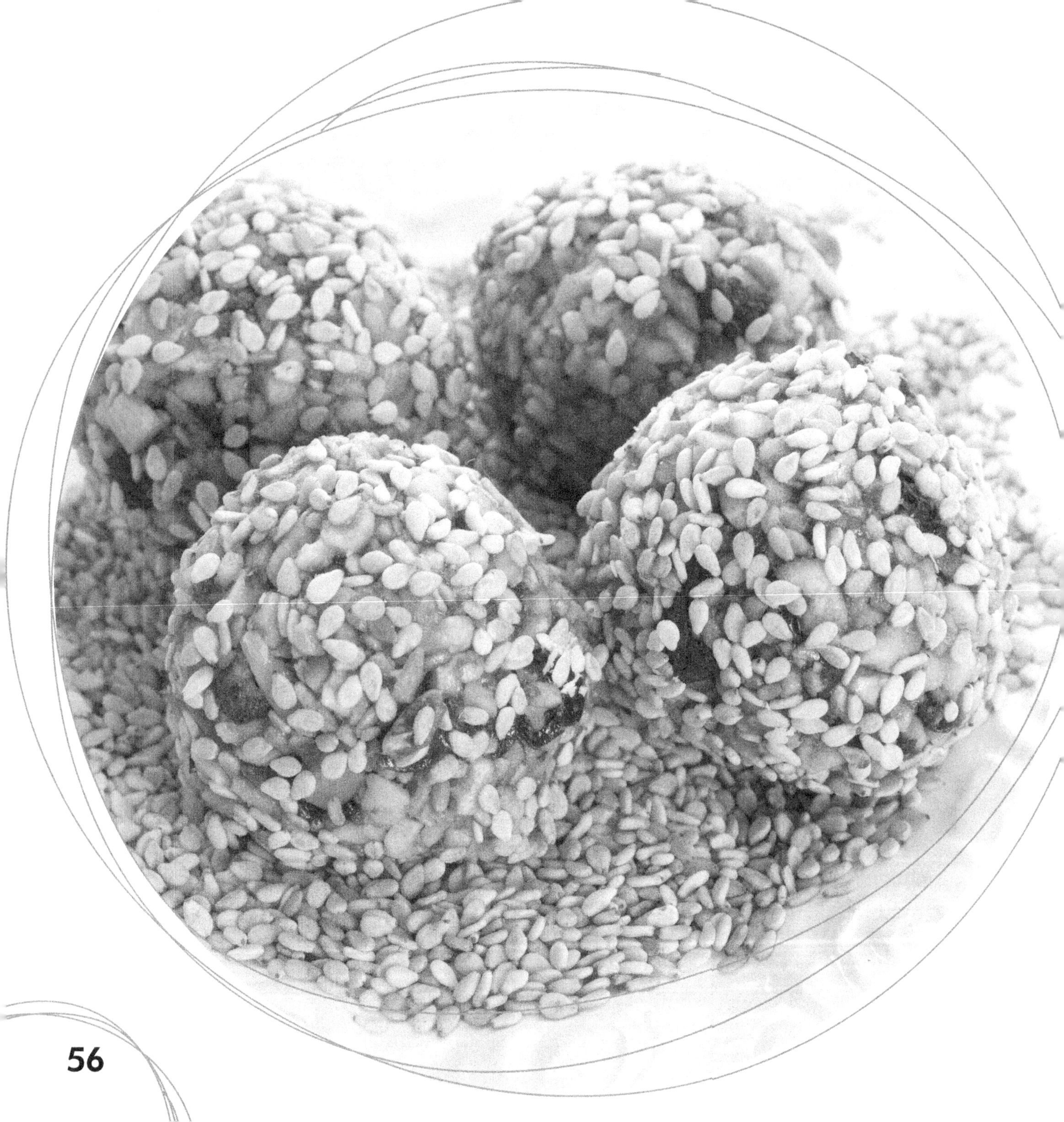

Pistachio & Sesame Superpower Bites

Ingredients

150g (5oz) pistachio nuts
125g (4oz) oats
100g (3½ oz) peanut butter
25g (1oz) 100% cocoa powder or cacao nibs
1 teaspoon maca powder
1 teaspoon ground cinnamon
1 tablespoon tahini paste (sesame seed paste)
2 tablespoons honey
2 tablespoons water (optional)
Pinch of salt
Sesame seeds for rolling

Method

Place the oats and nuts in a food processor and blitz until roughly chopped. Transfer them to a large bowl and add in the maca, cocoa powder or cacao nibs, cinnamon, peanut butter, tahini paste (sesame seed paste) and honey. Mix it well then add a pinch of salt. Add a tablespoon or two of water if the mixture seems a bit dry to stick together. Shape the mixture into balls. Scatter some sesame seeds on a plate and roll the balls in them. Chill them for at least an hour before serving.

Macadamia & Coconut Bites

MAKES approx. 24

Ingredients

125g (4oz) almond butter
75g (3oz) desiccated (shredded) coconut
75g (3oz) macadamia nuts, chopped
2 tablespoons tahini paste (sesame seed paste)
1 teaspoon stevia sweetener (or more to taste)
Extra coconut for rolling

Method

Place the coconut, tahini (sesame seed paste), almond butter and chopped macadamia nuts into a bowl and combine them thoroughly. Stir in a teaspoon of stevia powder then taste to check the sweetness. Add a little more sweetener if you wish. Roll the mixture into balls. Scatter some desiccated (shredded) coconut on a plate and coat the balls in it. Keep them refrigerated until ready to use.

Beetroot Falafels

Ingredients

150g (5oz) uncooked chickpeas (garbanzo beans)
150g (5oz) cooked beetroot, peeled and diced
1 teaspoon paprika
1 tablespoon fresh coriander (cilantro) leaves, finely chopped
1 clove of garlic, finely chopped
1 teaspoon chia seeds
½ teaspoon bicarbonate of soda
Zest of 1 lemon

Method

Steep the chickpeas (garbanzo beans) in water overnight. Boil the chickpeas (garbanzo beans) for around 1 hour until they have softened then drain them and allow them to cool. (Alternatively, you can use tinned chickpeas (garbanzo beans). Place the cooked beetroot and chickpeas into a blender and process until smooth. Add in the lemon zest, paprika, coriander (cilantro), chia seeds, garlic and bicarbonate of soda. Shape the mixture into balls and spread them out on a greased baking tray. Transfer them to the oven and cook at 180C/360F for 20 minutes. Serve warm or cold.

Broad Bean Bites

Ingredients

150g (5oz) broad beans
1 small red onion, chopped
1 red chilli, chopped
1 garlic clove, crushed
1 teaspoon spirulina
1 teaspoon ground allspice

Method

Place all of the ingredients into a food processor and blend the mixture to a smooth paste. Scoop out the mixture and shape it into balls. Lightly grease a baking tray and lay out the broad bean bites. Transfer them to the oven and bake at 180/360F for 20 minutes.

Chia & Mushroom Savoury Balls

Ingredients

200g (7oz) button mushrooms
150g (5oz) walnuts, chopped
75g (3oz) puy lentils
2 tablespoons chia seeds
2 cloves of garlic, chopped
1 handful of fresh chives
1 handful of fresh coriander (cilantro)
2 tablespoons soy sauce

Method

Soak the chia seeds in water for 5 minutes. In the meantime cook the lentils according to the instructions. Place the mushrooms and soy sauce in a frying pan and cook for 6 minutes or until the mushrooms have softened. Place the cooked lentils, chia seeds, mushrooms, walnuts, garlic, chives and coriander (cilantro) into a blender and blitz until smooth. Shape the mixture into balls. Place the balls onto a lightly greased baking sheet. Transfer them to the oven and cook at 180C/360F for 20 minutes. These delicious versatile snacks can be eaten hot or cold or even added to salads and pasta dishes.

Fresh Herb & Spicy Sweet Potato Cakes

Ingredients

150g (5oz) cannellini beans
2 sweet potatoes, peeled and chopped
2 teaspoons ground coriander (cilantro)
2 teaspoons ground cumin
2 cloves of garlic, peeled
Large handful of fresh coriander (cilantro) leaves
Large handful of fresh chives
1 tablespoon olive oil

Method

Steam the sweet potato until soft and tender. Set it aside until it cools down. Place all of the ingredients, apart from the olive oil, into a food processor and blitz until everything is combined. Shape the mixture into patties then place them in the fridge for an hour to become firm. Grease a baking tray with the olive oil. Place the sweet potato cakes onto the tray and bake in the oven at 220C/440F for around 15 minutes or until slightly golden.

Kale & Cannellini Bean Balls

Ingredients

250g (9oz) cannellini beans, drained
125g (5oz) kale, finely chopped
2 tablespoons ground almonds
1 tablespoon tahini paste (sesame seed paste)
1 tablespoon maca powder
1 tablespoon lemon juice
1 egg
1 teaspoon fresh parsley

Method

Place the kale in a steamer and cook for around 6 minutes or until it has softened. Allow the kale to cool then place all of the ingredients into a blender. Blitz the ingredients until the mixture is smooth. Shape the mixture into ball shapes and place them in on a lined baking tray. Cook them in the oven at 180C/360F for 25 minutes.

Spiced Quinoa & Chickpea Falafels

Ingredients

400g (14oz) tin of chickpeas (garbanzo beans)
200g (7oz) quinoa, cooked
3 spring onions (scallions), finely chopped
2 teaspoons ground coriander (cilantro)
1 stalk of celery, finely chopped
1 teaspoon ground turmeric
1 tablespoon chickpea flour (garbanzo bean flour)
½ red pepper (bell pepper), finely diced
2 tablespoons water (optional)
2 tablespoons olive oil
Juice of ½ lemon

Method

Place the chickpeas (garbanzo beans) into a blender and process until smooth then transfer it to a large bowl. Heat the olive oil in a frying pan, add the spring onions (scallions), red pepper (bell pepper), coriander (cilantro) and celery and cook it for 5 minutes until they have softened. Add them to the bowl with the chickpeas. Add in the quinoa, chickpea flour (garbanzo bean flour), turmeric and lemon juice and mix until all of the ingredients are thoroughly combined. Shape the mixture into bite-size balls. You can wet your hands slightly and/or add a tablespoon or two of water to the mixture to help shape it. Lay them out on a greased baking tray. Transfer them to the oven and bake at 180C/360F for 20 minutes or until golden.

Kale & Chickpea Bites

Ingredients

400g (14oz) tinned chickpeas (garbanzo beans)
150g (5oz) kale, finely chopped
3 cloves of garlic, crushed
2 tablespoons tahini (sesame seed paste)
2 tablespoons fresh squeezed lemon juice
¼ teaspoon ground cumin
¼ teaspoon chilli powder
¼ teaspoon sea salt
¼ teaspoon black pepper
1 tablespoon ground almonds
1 teaspoon olive oil

Method

Place the chickpeas (garbanzo beans), kale, tahini (sesame seed paste), garlic, lemon juice, chilli powder, cumin, salt and pepper into a food processor and blend until the mixture is smooth. Stir in the ground almonds and mix thoroughly. Scoop the mixture into ball shapes. Grease a baking sheet with olive oil and place the balls on the sheet. Transfer them to the oven and bake at 190C/375F for 25 minutes, turning the balls once halfway through cooking. Allow them to cool slightly before serving.

Made in the USA
Monee, IL
19 December 2022